KNOW-IT-ALL GUIDES

CONQUERING ROMANS

Nigel Crowle

Illustrated by Martin Chatterton

PUFFIN

PUFFIN BOOKS

Published by the Penguin Group
Penguin Books Ltd, 80 Strand, London WC2R 0RL, England
Penguin Group (USA) Inc., 375 Hudson Street, New York, New York 10014, USA
Penguin Group (Canada), 90 Eglington Avenue East, Suite 700, Toronto,
Ontario, Canada M4P 2Y3 (a division of Pearson Penguin Canada Inc.)
Penguin Ireland, 25 St Stephen's Green, Dublin 2, Ireland
(a division of Penguin Books Ltd)
Penguin Group (Australia), 250 Camberwell Road, Camberwell, Victoria 3124,
Australia (a division of Pearson Australia Group Pty Ltd)
Penguin Books India Pvt Ltd, 11 Community Centre, Panchsheel Park,
New Delhi – 110 017, India
Penguin Group (NZ), cnr Airborne and Rosedale Roads, Albany, Auckland 1310,
New Zealand (a division of Pearson New Zealand Ltd)
Penguin Books (South Africa) (Pty) Ltd, 24 Sturdee Avenue, Rosebank,
Johannesburg 2196, South Africa

Penguin Books Ltd, Registered Offices: 80 Strand, London WC2R 0RL, England

www.penguin.com

First published 2005
1

Text copyright © Nigel Crowle, 2005
Illustrations copyright © Martin Chatterton, 2005
All rights reserved

The moral right of the author and illustrator has been asserted

Set in Bookman Old Style
Made and printed in England by Clays Ltd, St Ives plc

Except in the United States of America, this book is sold subject to the condition
that it shall not, by way of trade or otherwise, be lent, re-sold, hired out, or otherwise circulated without the publisher's prior consent in any form of binding or
cover other than that in which it is published and without a similar condition
including this condition being imposed on the subsequent purchaser

British Library Cataloguing in Publication Data
A CIP catalogue record for this book is available from the British Library

ISBN -10: 0–141–31972–0
ISBN - 13: 978–0–14131–972–8

Just as Rome wasn't built in a day, this book wouldn't have been possible without the constant support and inspiration of those two Pillars Of The Crowle Empire: all hail the Empress Melanie, my wife, and Siônus Maximus, son and gladiator.

This tablet of stone is also dedicated – with appropriate salutations – to Mater and Pater (that's posh Latin words for my mum and dad), who've been a civilizing influence throughout my life and have praised me ever since I wore my first toga!

Huge thanks to those impressive Roman Generals, Jane, my editor, and Sarah, my agent, for their advice and help in making this book essential reading matter at the local bathhouse.

Thanks also to trusty foot soldiers Fiona, Liam, Trisha and Andrew, who lent me reference books to gather these facts. To thank the individual authors of those books would take longer than building Hadrian's Wall, but I'm grateful to all of them for directing me along particular avenues and aqueducts of research.

Look at the top right-hand corner of every page and
you'll see me.
Flick the pages and watch me march!

Contents

So, You Want To Know About . . . Those Conquering Romans

'Friends, Romans, Countrymen. Lend me your ears . . .'

That's a famous quote from Shakespeare's play, *Julius Caesar*, and it basically means, 'Hey there! Listen up!' That's because I want to ask you a question. Here it is.

'What have the Romans ever done for us?'

Well, for one thing, they have inspired this book! So flick through its pages, and learn all sorts of gob-smackingly unbelievable yet totally true stuff you never knew you never knew about gladiators, emperors, gods, athletes and the like . . .

It's packed full of quickie quizzes and fascinating facts about life way back then – which started around 753 BC and ended around AD 476.

However, be warned – every chapter, you'll find one fact that is complete tosh. An out-and-out lie. An outrageous falsehood. An exaggerated, falsified, fabricated, phoney, deceptive, whopping great whopper, in fact!

That's your challenge – can you Find That Fib? Read on, dear readers . . .

ROMANS – Timeline

The Roman Monarchy, 753 BC to 509 BC

BC	
753	Rome is founded
600	The Forum is built
578	First sewer is built
509	The Romans get quite annoyed with the meanness of their king with the silly name – Tarquinius Superbus – and get rid of the monarchy
450	First written Roman law appears and is known as the Twelve Tables
378	Rome becomes the ruling power in Italy
326	The Circus Maximus is built
312	The first aqueduct is built
280	Coins first appear
272	Rome gains control of the whole of Italy
264–241	Rome defeats Carthage in the First Punic War. Rome takes Sicily
264	First gladiatorial games are fought

218–201	Rome wins the Second Punic War and defeats Hannibal of Carthage and his elephants. Spain comes under Roman rule
149–146	Carthage is destroyed in the Third Punic War, and Africa becomes part of the Roman empire
148–133	Macedonia and Asia are taken over by Rome
149	Battle of Corinth, and Rome conquers Greece
73	Spartacus leads the gladiators in a revolt
49	Caesar becomes Dictator
47	Caesar invades Egypt and makes Cleopatra Queen
55	The Julian Calendar is invented
44	Caesar is killed
31	Augustus becomes the very first emperor of Rome
30	Cleopatra kills herself with a bunch of snakes and Egypt is taken over by Rome
AD 1	The population of Rome increases to 1 million
14	Augustus kicks the bucket and Tiberius becomes Emperor

25	Emperor Marcus Vipsanius Agrippa builds the Pantheon
37	Tiberius dies and Caligula becomes Emperor
41	Caligula's insanity gets on everyone's nerves and he is assassinated. Claudius becomes Emperor
43	Claudius invades and begins the Conquest of Britain
49	London is founded by the Romans in Britain
54	Claudius is succeeded by the nasty Nero
60-61	Queen Boudicca leads a revolution against the Romans in Britain. She is unsuccessful and kills herself
64	Nero throws a tantrum and burns down Rome
79-80	Mount Vesuvius erupts and Pompeii is destroyed. The Colosseum is completed
122	The Emperor Hadrian builds his wall across northern England to protect it from the barbarians
161	Marcus Aurelius becomes Emperor
300	The population of the Roman Empire is now 60 million people

312-313	Constantine becomes Emperor
324	The new city of Constantinople is founded (now Istanbul)
337	Constantine dies and the Roman Empire is split into two
380	The Roman Empire converts to Christianity
410	Germanic troops begin attacking the empire. Roman troops pull out of Britain to defend Rome
451	Huns invade Italy
476	The last Roman emperor is forced to give up his leafy crown and retire. This is essentially the end of the western Roman empire

km 0   500

m 0   400

Pannonia

Dacia

Dalmatia   Moesia

Thracia   Pontus   Armenia

Bithynia   Sophene

Macedonia   Galacia   Cappadocia

Epirus   Osroene

Asia

Achaea   Lycaonia   Syria

Cilicia

Cyprus

Pisidia   Judea

Lycia

Pamphylia

Cyrenaica   Arabia Petraea

1. Life and Death in Ancient Rome

How many times have adults said to you, 'Tchh! You kids today, you've got such an easy life. Why, when I was your age . . .' (Insert Something Really Strange, like: '. . . I had to eat coal instead of fancy breakfast cereal!' or '. . . we didn't waste money on flashy shoes, we wore the shoeboxes instead!')

Well, times really were tough in Ancient Rome. And it's about to get tougher – can you Find That Fib?

wife and
Imperial
Rome
to support

Everyday Life

A typical day in the life of an ancient Roman citizen began at dawn. Breakfast was just one cup of water. (Mmmm! Tasty!) Then it was off to the barber's shop for a quick shave with an iron razor . . . and a chance to catch up on all the latest gossip.

Of course, Roman ladies didn't need to shave (well, not regularly . . .), so they had to wait till they could lounge around at the public baths in order to dish the dirt and have a good gossip.

Top Three Nicknames for People in Ancient Rome
(in order of politeness)

3.
Flaccus — for someone who is fat and flabby.

2.
Naso — for someone who has a big nose.

1.
Maximus — for someone who is the greatest

BEST INSULT

Fathers had total power in a Roman household. They could condemn their slaves, their servants, their wives and even their children to death if they felt like it. Think about that next time you're cheeky to your dad!

When we think of the Romans, we imagine glamorous, marble-columned villas, but in a city like Rome only the wealthy could afford a single family house or *domus*.

The middle classes and the poor lived in far less swanky conditions – often in three- to six-storey, badly built blocks of flats called *insulae* (or 'island housing').

These wooden death traps were not only on the point of collapse, they also caught fire easily.

That was because:

(a) Ancient Rome was plagued by fireflies;
or
(b) Everyone burnt oil in lamps, torches and candles;
or
(c) Roman emperors had fiery tempers.

The answer is, of course, (b).

Just as it is today, shopping was a popular Roman pastime. The Emperor Trajan built the first shopping mall on several levels. Called the Markets of Trajan, it comprised over 150 different outlets, selling all sorts of stuff, from silks to spices and from farm implements to foodstuffs.

Keeping Clean

In the early years of their empire, the Romans weren't very keen on bathing – and would go for ages without having a good scrub-down. However, when they worked out a way of heating the water and air in their public baths, bathing became the hub of Rome's social life. In the Baths of Caracalla, around 1,600 bathers could get a massage, swim in the pool, work out at the gymnasium, or soak in a warm-water bath.

How to Take a Roman Bath

1) Take a Hot Bath

2) Take a Dry Bath

3) Take a Warm Steam Bath

4) Take a Deep Breath . . .

5) Take a Cold Plunge!

The Main Parts of a Typical Public Baths in Rome

Tepidarium —
the warm room

Calidarium — the
hot room

Frigidarium — the
cold room

Unctuaria — rooms
where people had their
skin oiled and scraped

There were also rooms for Sweating and Dressing.

Love and Marriage

Different Kinds of Kissing in Rome

The Romans were passionate about puckering up. They used to kiss each other hello, kiss their leaders' finger rings and robes, and kiss the statues of their gods to show their respect. In fact, they kissed so much, they also gave names to different degrees of smooching.

Top Three Ancient Roman Kisses

3. *osculum* — a kiss between friends

2. *basium* — a kiss between two people who really love one another

1. *savium* — a kiss with tongues . . . yuck!

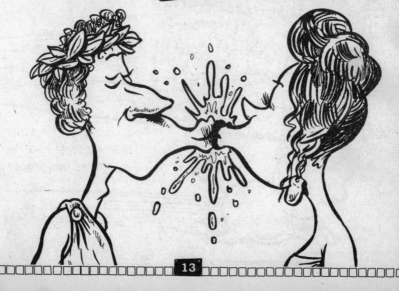

Ten Steps to Finding True Love in Ancient Rome:

1. Parents of 14- to 15-year-old girl match-make to find suitable husband.

2. At ceremony, bride wears an orange-coloured veil. Her hair is divided into six locks by the point of a spear and held in place by ribbons.

3. Pig is sacrificed in bride's home, or at shrine.

4. Bride and groom exchange vows, and the union is sealed not with a kiss but by holding hands.

5. Bride and groom lead procession to groom's house.

6. Bride smears fat and oil on doorposts to show that the house will never want for food in future.

7. Bride adds woollen wreaths to doorposts, as symbols of her future work as mistress of the household.

8. Bride drops first of three coins she carries as an offering to god of the crossroads, gives second coin to new hubbie, and third coin is offered to god of house.

9. Groom scatters sesame-seed cakes, sweetmeats and nuts through the crowd.

10. Bride is carried through doorway by groom, who gives her fire and water as a token of their forthcoming life together.

Bridal Traditions

Once a Roman bride had lit a fire in the hearth of her new home, she would then throw a token to her wedding guests. However, unlike wedding ceremonies today, it wouldn't be a floral bouquet she'd throw. No, she'd fling the torch itself, and guests would scramble to be the first to grab it. Presumably a bride would wait until the torch had gone out before chucking it over her shoulder . . . otherwise there wouldn't be a burning desire to grab it!

Death in Rome

At the very moment when a Roman died, Charun, the leader of the evil guardian spirits, would have an almighty tussle with the goddess Vanth (who represented the good spirits) as Good and Evil wrestled to grab the soul of the poor deceased person. The newly dead then travelled to the afterworld by chariot, on horseback or on foot, depending upon how good they'd been in life.

Wealthy Romans made wax masks and busts of their dead ancestors and displayed them in their halls. If there was a family death, the family member who most resembled the dearly departed ancestor not only wore their death mask but also dressed in clothing appropriate to that relative's rank. Creepy, or what?

In 44 BC, Julius Caesar ignored a soothsayer's advice to 'Beware the Ides of March!' (Modern translation – 'Pull your duvet over your head and stay in bed all day on the 15th of March') and went to the Senate as usual. Unfortunately, a bunch of assassins with freshly sharpened daggers were already waiting there, and turned poor Julius into a human pincushion! He was stabbed 23 times, by friends and colleagues.

Dying, Roman-style.

CREEPIEST TRADITION

The funeral procession of an important Roman was sometimes enlivened by the appearance of a stilt-walker blowing a two-metre-long brass trumpet – a practice intended to summon mourners to the graveside, where they were treated to a traditional upbeat song-and-dance routine – still on stilts.

DID YOU FIND THAT FIB?

2. Rome wasn't Built in a Day

Whether they were ordinary homes or magnificent temples, the Romans were proud of their skill at building buildings. But Rome wasn't built in a day... Don't forget, there's one obvious whopper among the following selection – can you Find That Fib?

The Colosseum (AD 80)

On the site of the hated Emperor Nero's palace and park, the Colosseum was built by the military leader Vespasian.

Colosseum: Vital Statistics

- it measured 188 X 156 metres and was 50 metres high
- the arena measured 86 X 54 metres
- it was made up of four levels of arcades
- it needed 292,000 cartloads of stone, taken from nearby Tivoli
- it was held together by 300 tonnes of iron

building only took ten years to build. It held 50,000 spectators and advertised spectacles such as crucifixions and beast hunts. Artificial lighting (the Roman equivalent of floodlights) was used to brighten proceedings for spectators during dark December days.

9,000 animals had been slaughtered at the Colosseum's opening event alone.

Wild animals were kept in cages under the arena, only to be let out to be slaughtered or to fight one another.

BLOODIEST BUILDING

To celebrate Trajan's triumph in the Second Dacian War, guess how many beasts were killed.

(a) 100?

(b) 1,000?

(c) 11,000?

The answer, sadly, is (c), 11,000.

The Forum (from 200 BC)

From around 200 BC, the southern marketplace area of the Forum started to come into its own as a location for the first fashion shows held in the city. Citizens vied with one another in a competition to find the 'Finest Roman Toga', which was modelled by the youngest girl in a family. These young models had to watch their step as they strutted their stuff along a 'catwalk' made of wood and marble. The walkway was only 20 centimetres wide, and if anyone lost their footing, they'd fall a metre and a half to the ground!

The Pantheon (27 BC–AD 300)

The Romans couldn't leave this temple to their gods alone.

In 27 BC, Marcus Vipsanius Agrippa began building the Pantheon.

The Emperor Hadrian completely rebuilt it between AD 118 and 128 and, around AD 300, the Emperors Lucius Septimius Severus and Caracalla added a bit too.

The dome is an impressive 43 metres in diameter, and is also 43 metres above its base. It is still standing in all its glory today.

The Circus Maximus
(from 329 BC)

Tarquin, Rome's first Etruscan king, held the first Roman games (consisting of boxing and racing) on a site which became the Circus Maximus. This was the first and largest *circus* (a place for chariot races) in Ancient Rome. Chariot races were staged in this oval-shaped stadium which had a barrier splitting it in half along the middle.

Hadrian's Wall (AD 122–130)

Hadrian became Roman Emperor in AD 117 and ruled for 21 years. He loved travelling and he visited all his provinces, causing him to be away from Rome for years at a time.

Although built in Britain, Hadrian's Wall is perhaps the most powerful symbol of the once mighty Roman Empire. The wall ran for 73 English miles (117 kilometres) from Britain's east coast at Wallsend-on-Tyne to Bowness-on-Solway in the west. Taking six years to build, it was intended to separate the Romans from the barbarians – that is, the unconquered Caledonians of Scotland. The wall was six metres high and three metres across at its widest point.

Hadrian's Wall was originally painted white

At every Roman mile stood a milecastle, guarded by soldiers and with two turrets where sentries kept watch. This was so the Romans could keep a close check on the movement of goods, people and animals crossing the frontier.

Pompeii (AD 79)

OK, a town isn't strictly a building, but the tragedy of Pompeii has helped shape our understanding of the buildings of Ancient Rome.

Mount Vesuvius – a volcano that everyone thought was extinct – suddenly erupted into life, shooting out thousands of tonnes of boiling lava.

The town of Pompeii was buried under four metres of volcanic ash. A tenth of the town's population – that's 2,000 people – lost their lives in the disaster. The volcanic eruption buried the nearby town of Herculaneum under a 20-metre-deep mudflow that completely covered all the buildings. Neither town was ever lived in again – in fact, they were forgotten about until the sixteenth century.

In the eighteenth century, a great deal of Pompeii, and some of Herculaneum, was dug up. These discoveries gave us a unique glimpse into Roman life as the excavators found whole buildings and corpses left intact. A more gruesome picture emerged as the victims' bodies rotted away in the air, and plaster was poured into the holes left in the ash. Some extremely detailed models were created – even down to the sandals and clothes the unfortunate inhabitants had been wearing.

Top Five Bits of Graffiti Scrawled on Walls by Ordinary Romans in Old Pompeii (in order of stupidity):

5.
'Lovers, like bees, live a life —— I wish!'

4.
'On honeyed 19 April, I baked bread'

3.
'Gaius Julius Primigenius was here. Why are you late?'

2.
'Comicus Restius stood here with his brother'

1.
'I have a head cold'

UP POMPEII

DID YOU FIND THAT FIB?

3. Times of the Day and Year

Ah . . . the festival in ancient times! The Romans may not have had multiplex cinemas or stretch limos, but they knew how to throw a party! Mind you, some of the things they got up to would make your jaw drop! So, let's see if you have cause to celebrate as you Find That Fib amongst this lot.

The Roman Calendar

The Romans were so fond of their gods and their religion, they invented a calendar so that they could keep track of important festivals and events. By the first century BC, they followed the cycle of the moon, with only 355 days. As time passed, this meant that some festivals were often celebrated in the wrong season.

To stop the confusion, in 46 BC Julius Caesar issued an improved calendar of 365¼ days and a leap year every four years. These official calendars were used by the Romans as a timetable so that they'd know each year exactly when to worship their gods. It worked so well, our current Gregorian calendar is modelled upon it.

Caesar's ideal calendar!

I ♥ Fertility

I ♥ Protection

Top Eight Weird Roman Festivals

15 February – *Lupercalia*
This was an important fertility festival. Goats (symbols of fertility) and dogs (symbols of protection) were sacrificed. Then two young boys were led to the altar. Priests wearing goatskins would touch the boys' brows with a bloody knife, wiping it afterwards with wool soaked in milk. The priests, who were anointed in blood, would then run around, whipping onlookers with a goatskin whip.

28 April–3 May – *Floralia*
The Ancient Roman festival of flowers was intended to please the goddess Flora so that, in turn, she would protect blossoms. Happy Romans walked around with floral wreaths in their hair. However, the festival fell out of favour, and in 173 BC the Roman Senate reinstated the festival as *Ludi Florales*, a theatrical event which included mimes and naked actresses.

9–13 May – *Lemures*

In this festival, the Romans tried to persuade the spirits of the dead not to threaten the living. *Lemures* were supposed to be wandering spirits who threatened and terrorized those still alive.

On the 9, 11 and 13 of May, the heads of Roman households used to walk barefoot around their house at midnight, with a mouthful of dried black beans. As they walked, they spat out the beans one by one – the theory being that hungry spirits would gobble up the beans and leave the householders alone. To scare the spirits off, they would then bang pans together noisily. Spirits may have been greedy bean-gobblers, but they weren't fans of head-banging loud noise!

24 June – The Festival of Libertarius Maximus
On this day every year, everyone was allowed to wear a large fish, a lobster or a crab, on top of a flat hat, and dance around in praise of Libertarius, their god of fish, shellfish and crustaceans, and ancient provider of food from the sea.

25 July – *Furrinalia*
This festival was held in honour of everyone who searched for underground spring water. Romans mixed spring water with wine to toast the goddess of springs, Furrina. This was held during the season of drought, so the citizens could show how grateful they were for the underground springs.

23 August – *Vulcanalia*

During this festival, Romans celebrated Vulcan, the god of fire, and gave thanks for fire itself – celebrating both its useful and its destructive nature. It seems that Romans used to throw fish and other small animals into fires in order to preserve the human lives they represented.

4–17 November – *Ludi Plebii*

This festival of racing was celebrated with chariot races in honour of Jupiter Optimus Maximus, and was first established in 220 BC. It was one of a number of Roman feast days that were filled with a heady mix of theatrical events and racing. In the early days of the Empire, Romans celebrated 77 *ludi* or 'games days'. By AD 354, they'd set aside 175 days in the year for enjoying themselves.

17–23 December – *Saturnalia*

This Roman feast lasted for an amazing seven days. After a religious ceremony, those greedy Romans really made a meal of it, spending all day at the dining table. They took off their togas and ate wearing comfortable loose tunics. What's more, masters served their slaves who, for the duration of the festival, could do and say whatever they liked.

SLAVES' FAVOURITE WEEK

DID YOU FIND THAT FIB?

4. Growing Up

So, assuming that your dad has actually decided to keep you, what was it like growing up in Ancient Rome? Well, hopefully the following facts will give you some idea. But remember, one of these bits of trivia is an outright fib – the question is, can you spot which one?

School Daze

School was a privilege for rich kids, who were all brought up to dress, look and behave like mini versions of their mums and dads.

If you were poor, you were sent to work at an early age, and you grew up not knowing how to read or write.

Girls rarely received more than a basic education in Roman times. They went on to learn household skills, such as cooking and needlework, from their mothers.

Boys, on the other hand, attended school from daybreak until noon – and all children were thrashed if they hadn't learnt their lessons by heart.

Roman was his Name-o...

A freeborn male had three names. His first name (*praenomen*) marked him as an individual. His second name (*nomen*) denoted his clan (*gens*). His third name (*cognomen*) was either the same as his father's or differed from it on purpose. These third names were often drawn from nicknames, places of family origin, or occupation. Only his close friends would call him by his first name alone.

Popular First Names of Freeborn Roman Males

Sextus

Tiberius

Marcus

Quintus

Titus

Who says Ancient Romans thought Boys were Better than Girls?

In the early days of Ancient Rome, women and girls had no legal name. However (and possibly because Romans grew tired of addressing all passing females as 'Hey, you!') it became common practice to change the '-*us*' bit of a male name to '-*a*'. So, 'Iulius' became 'Iulia', and so on.

Popular First Names of Freeborn Roman Females

Ahhh. Right . . . Er . . . Not much point in doing this list, actually!

Games with nuts were popular with Roman youngsters – so much so that the phrase 'giving up your nuts' was used to describe the start of a child going to school. Except, of course, the Romans said it in Latin!

SILLIEST SAYING

Favourite Game Played by Roman Boys

Pretending to sacrifice goats at an altar, using hamsters in place of goats

Favourite Game Played by Roman Girls

Dressing up as your favourite goddess

Games Played by Roman Children

Hoopla
Knuckle bones
Dice
Spinning tops
Terracotta, clay or
Rag dolls
Lead models of animals
Rattles
Coin tossing
Marbles

Pets were starting to become popular in Roman times. Youngsters enjoyed playing with:

- dogs
- pigeons

- parrots

- quail
- ducks
- monkeys
(not widespread)
- cats
(only after 1st century AD).

When a young Roman male shaved for the first time, he put the bristles in a glass bottle, which he then offered to the gods, as thanks for having become a man.

WORST
OFFERING

Academia Roma Juniorius – Reportus Cardium

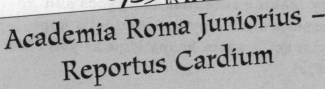

Gaius Maximus, age nine

Gaius is a pleasant lad who tries very hard, especially with his counting lessons on his abacus. However, he is not the neatest of pupils and has smudged quite a lot of his writing work on his wax tablet. Also, he needs to get to school on time — on several days last term he arrived just after daybreak. In science lessons, he enjoys any chance to cut open small animals, so I recommend that when he grows up, he tries to get a job as a sacrificial priest.

DID YOU FIND THAT FIB?

5.
Ye Gods

Your average Roman just wanted what we all want out of life: to be happy, and to be successful. To ensure this, they played it safe by making sure that their gods and goddesses were happy too. And let's hope that you get a warm happy glow as you Find That Fib!

Godly Payments

Romans didn't feel the need to worship or love these superhuman powers in the Greek way. They thought that their gods were there to protect people or groups, and the Romans paid them for their services with sacrifices.

Romans could be a bit uppity, though – if they didn't get value for money, they quickly stopped making payments and switched to worshipping another god . . .

> A 'sacrifice' means making an offering to God or the gods. Families usually offered small salty wheatcakes to their gods.

Keep it in the Family

Romans believed that their family lives were protected by a guardian god called Lar. A bride would cross the doorstep of her new house and immediately offer Lar a sacrifice and a coin. If someone died, two rams were sacrificed to Lar at the funeral so that the house remained pure.

A Roman God's New Year's Resolutions

1. Demand more sacrifices from pathetic Roman mortals (my supplies of spare ribs, chops and beefsteak are running low).

2. Pull strings to make sure mega-rich Titus Maximus's year goes well (he'll pay me in lots of oxen!).

3. Make sure mortals realize I'm *not* vegetarian; refuse to accept any more offerings of cheese, fruit or milk.

4. Spread rumour that Apollo is useless as a god (pick up all his sacrifices as well!).

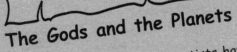

The Gods and the Planets

There's a tradition that scientists have named the planets in our solar system after various Roman and Greek gods — apart from Earth. Moons are generally named after minor gods who happen to be associated with the major ones.

Mercury: Roman god of travel, and closest planet to the sun — which is why it speeds faster through space than any other planet.

Venus: Roman goddess of love and beauty, and brightest of the planets known to the ancients.

Mars: Roman god of war, and known as the Red Planet.

Jupiter: Roman king of the gods, and more than twice as big as all the other planets combined.

Saturn: Roman god of agriculture, and second largest planet.

Uranus: Ancient Greek god of the heavens, the earliest supreme god, and third largest planet.

Neptune: Roman god of the sea, and fourth largest planet.

Pluto: Roman god of the underworld, and farthest, smallest planet from the sun.

Romans knew how to make a splash with a nifty name change.

Good God! You've Changed Your Name . . .

What is the difference between these Roman and Greek gods?

Roman		Greek	Roman		Greek
Jupiter	and	Zeus	Vulcan	and	Hephaestus
Venus	and	Aphrodite	Mercury	and	Hermes
Mars	and	Ares	Juno	and	Hera
Minerva	and	Athena	Saturn	and	Kronos
Ceres	and	Demeter	Neptune	and	Poseidon

Answer: Absolutely nothing! The Romans just 'borrowed' most of the Greek gods and gave them another name.

The Romans were such a religious nation, they decided that they needed a different god for every minute of every hour of the day. Sometimes they got so confused, they uttered the wrong name for the wrong god – and if anyone heard them doing this, the penalty was to have their tongue cut off. To try and prevent this before it happened, worried Romans even used to pray to Untidius, their god of confusion and mess.

What was the Roman God Apollo's name changed to?

(a) Domestos?
(b) Apollo?
(c) Eric?

Hey there, my name is Apollo and I'm pretty special...

Answer: (b) . . . er, actually, he remained Apollo – the only Roman god to have the same name as his Greek counterpart.

Roman Name Game

1.
Mars — both Roman god of war and a popular chocolate bar.

2.
Victoria — both Roman goddess of success in war and a type of sponge cake.

3.
Flora — both Roman goddess of budding springtime and a type of butter substitute.

DID YOU FIND THAT FIB?

Superstitions and Making Decisions

The Romans were great believers in the power of superstitions – and they'd have spent ages wondering what to do if they saw strange things. But can you see something strange in this collection and Find That Fib...

Animals as Sacrifices

For Ancient Romans, any sacrificial animal had to be perfect inside and out. If something was found to be wrong with its heart, liver or other organs, then the sacrifice was cancelled . . . and another animal had to be bought, prepared and slaughtered. Gradually, the people in charge became more expert at the job – or better liars!

Male animals were offered to gods and female animals to goddesses. You had to get the colour right too: black for underworld gods, and white for Juno and Jupiter. Red dogs were sacrificed to Robigus, the god who made crops grow properly. Other animals used in sacrifice were oxen, rams, boars, horses and goats.

Aw — what a pretty ox!

If you were rich and wanted to make a sacrifice to a heavenly god, you'd cap the tips of an ox's horns with gold – or, at the very least, tie ribbons to its horns.

When offering an ox, the slaughterer would slit its throat while holding the ox's head to face upwards. If an underworld god was being honoured, then the ox's head was held downwards.

If you're visiting modern-day Rome's church of Santa Maria, and people suspect you of lying, be very careful. They'll get you to repeat the lie once you've put your hand inside the *Bocca della Verità*, or Mouth of Truth. It's a stone carving of the sea god Oceanus and, if you really have lied, the jaws are supposed to snap shut on your fingers! However, some historians reckon it's nothing more than an ancient drain-covering that some Roman joker stuck on a wall.

Any amphibians in ancient times would do well to avoid hopping in front of a Roman soldier. Frogs were considered symbols of good luck in battle and were immediately speared by said soldier and proudly worn attached to the belt, provided the unfortunate frogs had been killed with just one quick stab.

FAVOURITE SACRIFICE

When Caligula was made Roman Emperor, how many cows were slaughtered and sacrificed at the Capitol over a period of three months?

(a) 16,000?   (b) 160,000?   (c) 1,600,000?

Answer: (b). The sacrifice-crazy emperor slaughtered 160,000 cows.

Romulus and Remus

Roman legend has it that when the founders of Rome, Romulus and Remus, decided to found a new city, the twins watched birds flying over different parts of the sky. Romulus saw 12 vultures, but Remus could see only six vultures, so Romulus reckoned that gave him the choice of a site, and he marked the boundary walls with a plough harnessed to a white cow and a white bull. Remus looked at the shallow furrow in the earth, sniggered and jumped over it. Looking back, that was a silly thing to do. It drove Romulus into a real stroppy mood and he killed his own brother!

Top Nine Strange Occurrences Noted by Roman Historian Livy During the Year 169 BC (in order of strangeness)

9. A spear burned for two hours without turning to ashes.
8. The sky seemed to be on fire.
7. A torch was seen in the sky.
6. A crested snake was seen in Rome's Temple of Fortuna.
5. It rained stones.
4. It rained blood.
3. A palm tree grew in the stone forecourt of a temple.
2. The statue of Apollo wept for three days and three nights.
1. A cow talked.

When making important decisions, such as declaring war, holding an assembly or passing a law, a Roman magistrate would watch for birds flying and singing in various quarters of the sky. Then a blindfolded 'augur' or interpreter would say what the augury signs meant.

Raven, crow and owl gave their signs by birdsong, while the eagle and vulture's flight paths foretold good or bad fortune.

The Sacred Chickens

In Roman times, sacred chickens were used to reach quick answers to questions. Special handlers – or *pullarii* – carried sacred chickens around in cages, even on the battlefield. They'd throw a piece of cake in front of the open cage door and watch what the sacred chicken did.

Good Signs

sacred chicken eats cake

bits of cake fall from beak of sacred chicken

Bad Signs

sacred chicken refuses to eat cake

sacred chicken flaps wings

sacred chicken cackles

sacred chicken flies away

One great story about the sacred chickens concerns a Roman general called Claudius Pulcher. During the First Punic War, he wanted to march to war, but decided to get a second opinion from the sacred chickens. When the sacred chickens refused to eat, the angry general threw them into the River Tiber, yelling, 'Well, let them drink!' Then he marched his men off on an expedition . . . which, you've guessed it, ended in disaster. He really should've listened to those sacred chickens!

Romans didn't only try to predict the outcome of battles. Sometimes, while making a journey, the head of the family would try to predict whether that journey would be successful, based upon seeing unusual things along the way. (It's a bit like asking Mum or Dad during a boring car ride, 'Are we nearly there yet?') Anyway . . .

Unusual Signs that Made Romans Pause for Thought include:

- the sudden appearance of pregnant dogs or foxes
- a wild wolf in the road
- the cry of an owl
- a snake crossing their path and frightening their horses
- flying birds, like woodpeckers or crows.

DAFTEST SUPERSTITIONS

DID YOU FIND THAT FIB?

7. Amazing Inventions

There's no getting away from it, the Romans were a smart bunch. Between them, they came up with all sorts of clever ideas, inventions and innovations that have totally changed our way of life. But are you clever enough to spot the fact about inventions that's been totally invented? Yes, of course you are . . .

The Romans invented central heating when they came up with the 'hypocaust', a floor raised on tile piers which was heated up by hot air circulating under it.

It was first used about 100 BC by the Romans for public baths. Later, it was introduced into private houses. Sometimes the floors and walls of the baths became so hot that bathers had to wear wooden clogs or risk burning their feet.

Top Three Things the Romans Discovered that Helped Humankind:

3.
roads (almost all of which lead to Rome, apparently).

2.
cross-bladed scissors (invented around AD 100)

1.
public toilets (By AD 315 Rome had 144 loos, all flushed clean by running water)

The Romans decided to make things a bit more interesting when it came to boxing matches, so they invented the *caestus*. They took a glove, weighed it down with lumps of iron, and then studded it with metal spikes. Seconds out . . . Round one! Ooh, painful . . . Call a doctor!

Hot Curls

Heated rollers were invented by the Romans. Women twisted their hair around a hollow tube, the inside of which was heated by a hot rod. (A 'hot rod' of metal, that is, not a 'hot rod' racing car, which wasn't invented till much later.)

'I have the Romans to blame for my racy hair-do!'

The Romans cleverly expanded their empire by controlling the water supplies, building channels called aqueducts. Ancient Rome had 11 major aqueducts, some supported by arched columns, the longest aqueduct being 95 kilometres long. The aqueduct helped expand the Roman Empire by bringing water to areas which were previously uninhabitable.

1 BA (Before Aqueducts)

With no toilet inside the poorer houses, Ancient Romans either used a potty or they could – for a small fee – use the world's first pay-per-sitting latrines. The poshest public loo had 20 seats built around a merrily spouting fountain, which made something of a conversation piece for toilet-goers.

Sculpted brackets in the form of leaping dolphins framed each marble toilet seat, which itself was:

(a) heated; or

(b) disinfected; or

(c) left standing in an upright position by the previous Roman male toilet-goer.

Answer: (a). Just as well, really – marble can be very cold to sit upon.

The Romans claim to have invented spectacles in the first century BC, when Emperor Nero used a cut jewel to see what was happening to his gladiators.

However, there is a much earlier statue of the Greek medical expert Hippocrates which shows him looking through the stem of a drinking glass.

The Emperor Augustus organized the world's first fire-fighters in Rome, around 2,000 years ago. They fought blazes with water pumps operated by hand and blankets soaked in vinegar.

When Vesuvius erupted, the volcano caused tremendous loss of life. However, some good did come out of the tragedy when the Romans discovered that you could mix the volcanic dust with lime and water. The resulting mix they called *caementum* – an early form of cement.

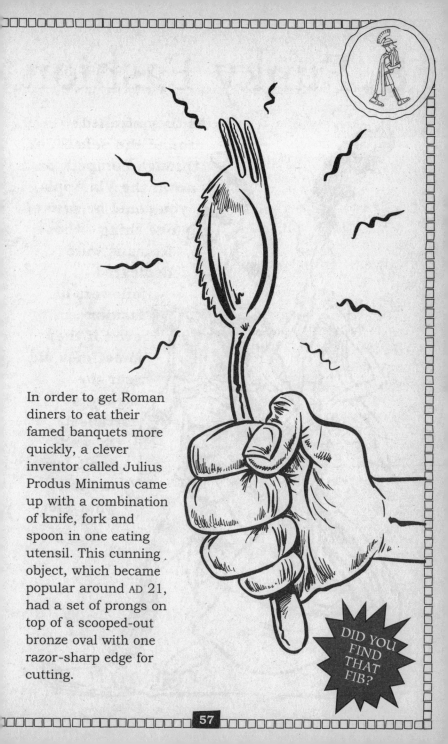

In order to get Roman diners to eat their famed banquets more quickly, a clever inventor called Julius Produs Minimus came up with a combination of knife, fork and spoon in one eating utensil. This cunning object, which became popular around AD 21, had a set of prongs on top of a scooped-out bronze oval with one razor-sharp edge for cutting.

DID YOU FIND THAT FIB?

8. Funky Fashion

As they strolled around the Senate, or through Pompeii, or down the Via Appia, you could be sure of one thing – those Romans were dedicated followers of fashion . . . even if they sometimes did wear the strangest articles! Oh, and don't forget to Find That Fib!

Rock-hard Hair

Hair was a big obsession of a typically fashionable Roman woman. Her hairdresser was called an *ornatrix*, and she used a framework of pins and combs to keep the lady's hair piled up on top of her head.

If the fashion-conscious female was rich enough to have sculpted busts made of herself, these were sometimes fashioned with removable stone wigs. This meant that the latest hairstyles could be fitted on top of the sculpture.

'My hairdresser's trapped inside my hairstyle too!'

MOST FASHIONABLE STATUES

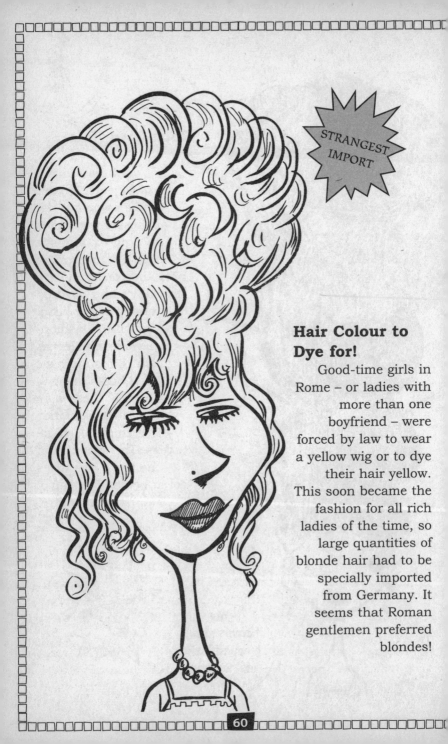

Hair Colour to Dye for!

Good-time girls in Rome – or ladies with more than one boyfriend – were forced by law to wear a yellow wig or to dye their hair yellow. This soon became the fashion for all rich ladies of the time, so large quantities of blonde hair had to be specially imported from Germany. It seems that Roman gentlemen preferred blondes!

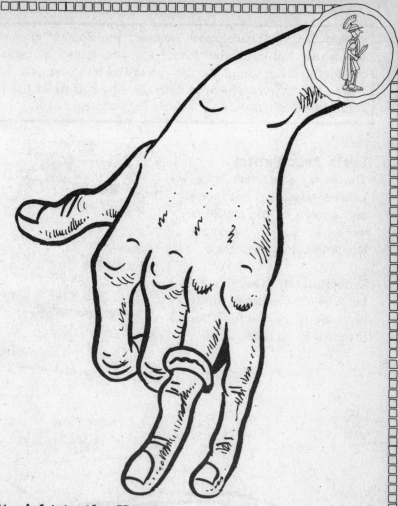

Straight to the Heart

The Romans began the custom of wearing wedding rings in the second century AD. Wives used gold signet rings to mark the household goods and protect them from light-fingered servants. A gold wedding ring (worn on the third finger of a woman's left hand) showed that a husband trusted his wife to manage his household.

Romans believed that the wedding ring finger (third finger, left hand) was special because a nerve ran straight from that finger to the heart.

In July 2003, archaeologists excavating a Roman temple on the south bank of the River Thames found a canister containing what could be the world's oldest cosmetic face-cream. It was even smeared with the fingerprints of the last Roman person who used it . . . over 2,000 years ago!

Let's Talk Pants!

There is some evidence, knicker-wise, that both men and women in Ancient Rome wore a simple wrapped loincloth under their togas.

Unfortunately there is no Latin word for boxer shorts, because they hadn't been invented in Roman times!

Four Roman Words for Underpants

1. *subligaculum* (meaning 'little binding underneath')
2. *subligar*
3. *cinctus*
4. *campestre*

Trying on Togas

Of course, the Romans were famous for wearing their togas. A toga was a heavy half-circle of wool which was wrapped over a tunic – or *tunica*. A toga wasn't the comfiest of outfits to wear or move about in, which is why a lot of citizens couldn't be bothered to wear them, even though going toga-less annoyed their emperors. Instead, they preferred to wear a *tunica* of wool or linen, over a shirt and loincloth. At meals, however, they'd sometimes wear a looser, coloured, lighter gown called a *synthesis*. By the third century AD, a long-sleeved tunic called a *dalmatica* had replaced the toga in popularity.

Your typical Roman slaves had to keep their hands and legs relatively free, in order to carry out their various tasks. That's why slaves just wore a *tunica* which was either fastened at the side with pins or (more usually) passed over the head.

The Emperor Augustus used to get so cold that he would often wear:
(a) four tunics; or
(b) the finest thermal underwear; or
(c) his mother's hand-made quilt, slung casually around his shoulders.

Emperor Augustus wishes he'd never tried to to chill out in his palace

Hippius Maximus makes his point at the senate

Make Our Roman Roads Groovy, Baby!

Campaigning Togas

If a Roman citizen wanted to campaign for a place in the Senate, he traditionally wore a particularly eye-catching coloured toga which was dyed in a swirl of shades – much in the style of the modern T-shirt worn by hippies. When wearing these togas of clashing bright pinks, brilliant oranges and deep purples, wannabe politicians would be easily recognizable in a crowd. It was a Roman tradition for their fellow citizens to then question them about their policies and beliefs.

Women's Clothes

Roman women wore a *stola* (or flowing garment) over their tunics, held in place at the waist with a belt. The *stola* was dyed red, saffron yellow or blue in colour.

Mosaics of the time show that Roman women also wore a modern-looking bra and pants, made of linen. These mosaics show that women at the gymnasium would keep in trim by lifting weights and throwing the discus while wearing Roman versions of a bikini.

Royal Togas

In Ancient Rome, you could always spot an emperor who'd just won a battle. Apart from the smug expression on his face, he'd be wearing a distinctive purple toga stained with a rare dye extracted from a purple shell called a *murex*. It seems that, in order to produce 1.4 grams of the purple dye – barely enough to dye a single Roman toga – workers had to crush 12,000 shells.

Kids' Togas

Roman children wore purple-edged togas until they reached adulthood, when they swapped over to a plain white toga. They also wore a *bulla* – a good-luck charm – around their neck until they grew up, to ward off evil spirits.

DID YOU FIND THAT FIB?

9. Roman Grub

If you wondered when you were going to get to the tasty bit of this book, then stop your stomach rumbling, because here it is! Feast your eyes on these facts, then Find That Fib, which should give you food for thought.

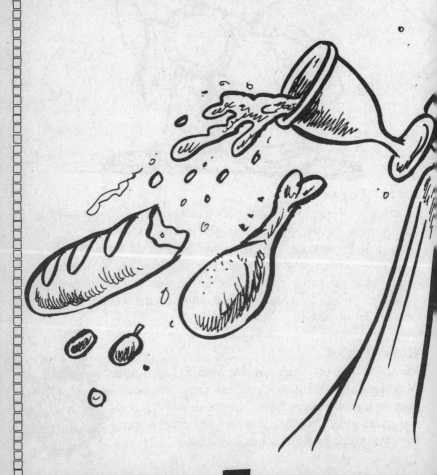

Eating like a Roman

Next time you're told off for messing around at mealtimes, casually drop the following fact into round-table conversation: Romans didn't use forks at meals, and – despite having spoons and knives – they didn't use them either. They preferred to use their fingers to eat their food off bright red pottery or silver plates.

Rich Roman greedy-guts would think nothing of sitting down to an eight-hour banquet, first guzzling snails swelled to bursting point on milk, then everything from wild boar, hare and dormice to ostriches, cranes and peacocks. They also imported 180 million litres of wine and 180 million litres of olive oil. In AD 300, there were 2,300 sellers of olive oil in Rome.

Things the Romans Did Eat at Meals

cereals (including bread)
vegetables (including
lettuce)
lentils
olives
eggs
figs
fish
pork

Things the Romans Didn't Eat at Meals

tomatoes
pasta
potatoes
bananas
oranges
sugar (honey was used to
sweeten things)
beef (well, hardly ever)

Mind you, most poor Romans ate bread and 'puls' – a porridge made of wheatmeal.

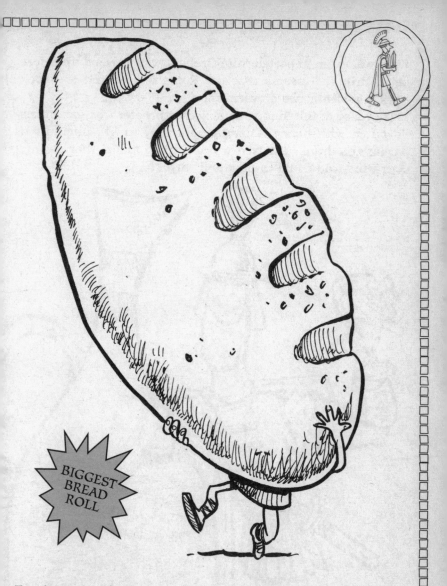

BIGGEST BREAD ROLL

To clean the dishes after meals, the Romans used to rub them in sand and rinse them off in clean water.

The Romans imported almost 200,000 tonnes of grain per year to make enough bread to see the people through any difficult periods, such as times of war, when supplies were limited, or during a famine.

Wine was often imported from Crete. It was warmed up before being drunk; it seems that the Romans preferred to knock back a goblet or two of warm wine.

They also drank their wine mixed with water – or sometimes flavoured with honey. They thought only rough, uncultured barbarians drank unmixed wine. If you'd tasted that strong, sour wine, you could understand why!

Three Uses of Olive Oil in Roman Times:

1. for cooking
2. for lighting
3. for bathing, in place of soap

A centurion's breastplate was to be found in most Roman kitchens, whether the family was involved with a military lifestyle or not. Women discovered that this piece of a soldier's uniform could be very useful when it came to grating cheese or peeling vegetables, as it yielded a more precise cutting edge than a knife.

MOST REVOLTING RECIPE

Recipe for Making Garum

1. Catch some small fish and place them in a vessel called an amphora.
2. Add the squidgy intestines of fish, e.g. mackerel, and oysters.
3. Cover with salt, blood and fishy juices.
4. Allow the amphora to heat up and go all smelly in the sun.
5. Open the amphora – and try not to be sick!

Those saucy Roman cooks were fond of making a stomach-churning mixture called *garum* – it was also known as *liquamen*. And it probably helped disguise the taste of food well past its sell-by date.

Vitellius was a legend among those food-stuffing, drink-swilling Roman emperors. He'd even stick a feather down his throat between courses to make himself sick. 'Tickling his palate' meant that the greedy emperor could make room for his next dish.

(Mind you, our own King Henry VIII's wife, Anne Boleyn, used to do the same thing – even at her coronation banquet. But at least her lady-in-waiting held up a sheet when the Queen looked likely to be sick at the table!)

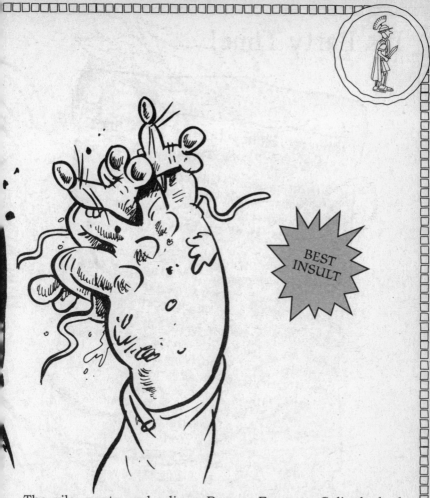

The vile, nasty and odious Roman Emperor Caligula had disgusting table manners. No, he didn't pick his nose. Instead, he would pick out criminals and instruct his favourite executioner to chop off their heads during dinner.

Dormice were specially bred in containers before being transferred to earthenware pots, where they were fattened up on chestnuts, walnuts and acorns. Before cooking, chefs used to stuff the poor creatures with pepper, pine kernels, minced pork and, of course, that tasty *garum* sauce.

It's Party Time!

Emperor Heliogabalus's Top Three Party Tricks

Roman Emperor Heliogabalus enjoyed entertaining himself at his dinner parties by playing cruel practical jokes on his guests. Here are his best ones:

3. He'd enjoy inviting, say, a group of hugely fat men to a meal and then laugh his head off as the poor porkers tried to squeeze on to the same couch together.

2. While he gorged himself at banquets, he'd serve his hapless guests inedible food made of wax, wood, ivory, earthenware, marble or stone. They'd have to play along with the joke, pretend to eat, and then wash their hands, while the greedy Emperor laughed and stuffed himself with real food.

1. He would shower down roses, violets and other flower petals from reversible ceilings. So many petals filled the banqueting rooms from floor to ceiling that the poor unsuspecting guests couldn't breathe, and some died.

Roman Party Bags

It seems it was the Romans who came up with the idea of a party bag for their guests at banquets. Hosts gave out pressies called *apophoreta*.

'Oooh, I hope I get a turnip!'

Party Bags Shopping List
truffles
turnips
birdcages
spoons
hairpins
bronze and clay sculptures

Some lucky banquet guests were even given take-away animals, like a donkey, a parrot, a swan or a pony.

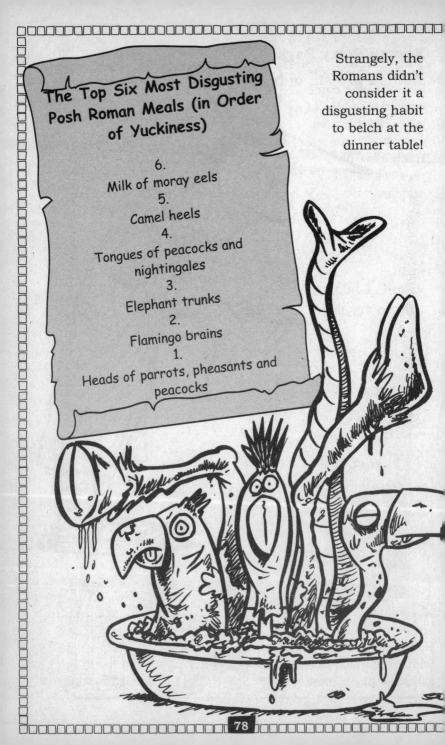

The Top Six Most Disgusting Posh Roman Meals (in Order of Yuckiness)

6.
Milk of moray eels
5.
Camel heels
4.
Tongues of peacocks and nightingales
3.
Elephant trunks
2.
Flamingo brains
1.
Heads of parrots, pheasants and peacocks

Strangely, the Romans didn't consider it a disgusting habit to belch at the dinner table!

The Priests' Feast, 70 BC (for top Roman priests only)

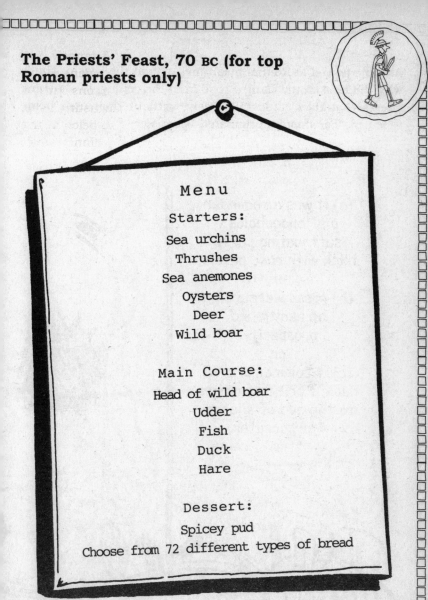

Menu

Starters:
Sea urchins
Thrushes
Sea anemones
Oysters
Deer
Wild boar

Main Course:
Head of wild boar
Udder
Fish
Duck
Hare

Dessert:
Spicey pud
Choose from 72 different types of bread

Although much was done by the host to take care of a guest's needs at a Roman banquet or even at an ordinary meal, each dinner guest was expected to bring his or her own napkin with them . . . How mean is that?

As wine flowed at Roman mealtimes, so did the gossip. That's why the host would hang a rose from the ceiling, to show the guests that they could talk freely, without their chat being repeated. The custom originated because:

(a) it was a reminder of Heliogabalus's suffocating party trick with rose petals;
or
(b) roses were a sign of health and prosperity;
or
(c) it commemorated Cupid's bribe of a rose to the god of silence, Harpocrates

DID YOU FIND THAT FIB?

Answer: (c). Cupid wanted to stop him spreading unsavoury stories about his mother, Venus.

10. Work, Work, Work

Unless you were stinking rich in Ancient Rome, you had to go out to earn an honest *denarius*. Now, though, it's your turn to go to work as you try to sort the fib from the facts among this lot.

Roman Currency

The basic unit of currency was the *as*, a coin made of bronze. A *denarius* was made from silver. An *aureus* was made from gold.

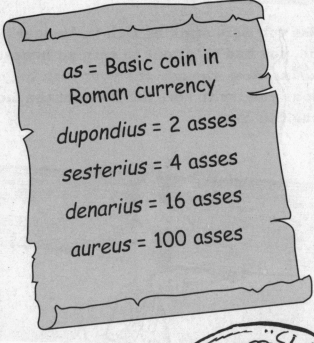

as = Basic coin in Roman currency

dupondius = 2 asses

sesterius = 4 asses

denarius = 16 asses

aureus = 100 asses

Eight *asses* would buy a Roman a small sack of wheat.

The typical annual wage of a Roman soldier was 225 *denarii*.

Coins pictured events such as Caesar's murder, as well as the heads of emperors.

Glass Work (if you can get it)

Although glass had been made for centuries, in the last century BC a Roman glassworker went beyond his job description when he found another use for the substance. Manlius Scipio discovered that by placing one piece of glass on top of another, he could direct the sun's rays to burn a hole in a piece of rag. Manlius may have come up with the idea for the first magnifying glass, but unfortunately he managed to burn down half his workshop in the process.

A *haruspex* worked for the emperor. Basically, he examined the liver and entrails of a sacrificed animal, then he foretold the future. Emperor Vitellius's *haruspex*, named Umbricus, foresaw a dangerous plot as he gazed at the blood and guts. Guess what? Emperor Vitellius was murdered that very day. Spooky, eh?

MOST GRUESOME JOB

Fast-Food Lovers

Here's a handy job in Ancient Rome: you could open your own fast-food outlet on the street. After all, everybody else cooked on the pavements.

Portable barbecues, stoves and braziers were an everyday feature of life among the poor of Rome, who became used to cooking out of doors.

In big cities like Rome, there were even early versions of our modern take-away restaurants, called *popinae*. These stalls sold cooked food for a few copper coins when the poor popped in at the *popinae*.

Saturn's Short Straw

As you know, even the gods had certain duties. Pity poor Saturn, then, who landed the prime job of:

(a) babysitting his little brother Pluto; or

(b) spreading manure on the fields; or

(c) going to the bar and buying a round of ambrosia for Mars and his mates.

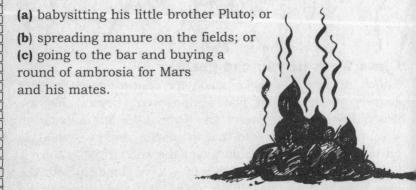

Answer: (b). Yuck! But it could've been worse – at least I used the word 'manure'!

Toilet Humour

Here's another of the most unpleasant jobs you could have in Roman times. The Emperor Vespasian turned a bankrupt Rome into a profitable city when he directed that the latrines' smelly 'end-product' (if you see what I mean) be collected, transferred to cisterns, taxed, and then sold to the guild of dry cleaners, who extracted the urine for cleaning clothes. Somebody (usually a slave) had to do all the transferring. Nice work if you can get it!

Slaves

You have to pity the poor slaves in Roman times – they had all the worst jobs to do, with none of the fun their masters and mistresses enjoyed. Furthermore, Roman slaves had to wear a disc – a bit like the one on the collar of a dog or cat.

The slave's name was written on this disc, together with his or her master's name and the address to which he or she should be returned, if caught on the run.

Then the poor slave had FUG – for *fugitivus* – branded on his or her forehead.

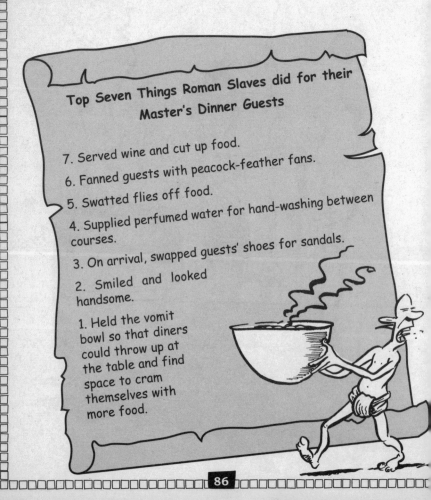

Top Seven Things Roman Slaves did for their Master's Dinner Guests

7. Served wine and cut up food.

6. Fanned guests with peacock-feather fans.

5. Swatted flies off food.

4. Supplied perfumed water for hand-washing between courses.

3. On arrival, swapped guests' shoes for sandals.

2. Smiled and looked handsome.

1. Held the vomit bowl so that diners could throw up at the table and find space to cram themselves with more food.

A fire-fighting Roman slave 'heads' for safety

Rome had seven fire brigades, but not a lot in the way of fire-fighting equipment. That's why the rich trained their slaves to rescue precious objects in the event of fire, which was fought with hand-pumps and buckets. But the slaveless poor often lost everything – including their lives.

Down at the Launderette

The 'fullers' of Ancient Rome did everyone's washing – but this, too, wasn't a pleasant job. First they had to heat up huge quantities of animal and human urine, then they sloshed it into baths and trampled on the dirty clothes to make them clean!

SMELLIEST JOB

DID YOU FIND THAT FIB?

11. That's Entertainment

After a hard day at the Senate, your average Roman liked nothing better than to sit with his fellow citizens, appreciating the finer things in life: a play, or a musical performance, or some poor soul being mauled to death by a lion in the middle of an amphitheatre! Can you relax enough to Find That Fib?

Top Three Ways of Applauding a Roman Play (in order of appreciation)

If you went to see a play in Roman times, you had a number of ways of showing how much you'd enjoyed the open-air spectacle.

1.
You could snap your finger and thumb together if you thought the play was merely OK.

2.
You could clap, obviously, if you thought it was a good play.

3.
However, if you wanted to rave about how great the play had been, you waved a handkerchief or the flap of your toga!

Mock Sea Battles

The Colosseum's arena was flooded by the Emperor Domitian so that mock seabattles called *naumachia* could be fought. Despite having laid special underfloor piping, the 'sea' -battle wasn't as spectacular as Domitian demanded. He went on to stage a series of these fake naval skirmishes on a much larger scale, as almost full-sized fleets fought it out on a huge artificial lake near the River Tiber. The poor sailors butchered one another until one side or the other was eliminated. Domitian was such a keen fan of these battles that even the heaviest rainstorm wouldn't stop him sitting through a naval contest.

The Gladiators

Retiarius
lone fighters, who fought
with fishing nets and
tridents

Samnites
who wore crested helmets
with face visors and
fought with short swords

**Other Types of
Gladiator
Secutor** – the
pursuer, had a
curved oblong
shield
Murrmillo – wore
a fish-like helmet
Provocator – the
challenger, wore
a protective
breastplate

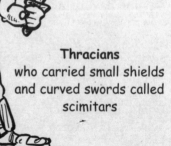

Thracians
who carried small shields
and curved swords called
scimitars

If you were a Roman gladiator, giving your all to avoid death in the amphitheatre, you would have appreciated a musical accompaniment to your efforts. Organists watched keenly as gladiators fought to the death, and made up musical pieces around those movements. Trumpeters and horn-blowers filled in with twiddly bits at dramatic moments in these real-life battles. Only loud instruments, such as organs, horns and trumpets, were suitable for such events.

Ancient Roman spectators could buy programmes – *libelli munerarii* – which included vital details about the top gladiators. Supporters could see at a glance how many times a particular gladiator had beaten an opponent (the letter 'V' for *victor*) or had fought well enough to leave the arena alive (the letter 'M' for *missus*).

Roman gladiators often wore armour made from the shell of the giant land tortoise. This made their fighting movements in the arena a little slow, but the tortoiseshell was surprisingly tough and protected gladiators from the blows of metal swords. Some gladiators would also stick ostrich feathers behind their ears as a lucky charm against defeat.

The Amphitheatres

The Roman emperors tried desperately to outdo one another with exhibitions of increasingly exotic wild animals. Roman audiences were impressed by a display of 300 ostriches, 200 stags, 200 ibexes (a type of mountain goat), 200 gazelles, 100 wild sheep, 100 wildcats, 100 bears, 30 wild horses, 150 boars and 10 elks. Beasts such as bears, elephants and hyenas were paraded around Roman amphitheatres before having to defend themselves to the death against the gladiators. Alternatively, they were set upon hapless slaves.

Later, the emperors came up with more crowd-pleasing spectacles to keep audiences entertained. These included elephants fighting bulls, lions fighting tigers or a bear being chained to a bull. Titus even ordered a female beast to be induced to give birth in the arena. What a charming lot those Romans were at times, eh?

'Civilized' Romans

Chariot Racing

Chariot racing was another popular form of entertainment. Chariots were drawn by four horses, in competition with up to 11 other chariots. Drivers didn't have someone waving a black-and-white chequered flag to mark the last lap of a race. Instead, they had to try and work out which lap they were on by watching officials in the centre of the track, who either:

(a) waved an old toga on a stick;

or

(b) blew a horn at full blast;

or

(c) upended a bronze dolphin on a set of outer rods, while removing an egg from a set of inner rods.

Answer: (c). Which is a bit more complicated than waving a black-and-white chequered flag at the fast approaching chariot drivers!

Winning the Race

There were four great chariot-racing teams, which were distinguished by their stables' colours: Reds, Greens, Whites and Blues. Many a bet was won or lost on a favourite – and the purple-and-gold-robed driver didn't even have to be hanging on to the reins of a winning chariot as it passed the finishing line. The dazed driver could have been flung in a heap on the ground, as even an empty chariot crossing the line meant his team could claim victory!

12. Wars and Battles

There's one thing you could always guarantee about Ancient Romans: they'd always be prepared to go to war in order to defend their opinions. But are you armed with the sort of knowledge to battle your way through this onslaught of fascinating facts, so that you can Find That Fib?

A Soldier's Life

Qualifications Romans had to Pass to Volunteer as Soldiers in Times Of War:

- be at least 1.73 metres tall
- be examined to ensure physical fitness
- have good eyesight
- sign on for 20 years.

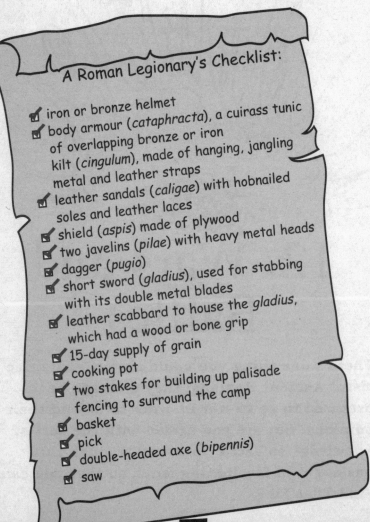

A Roman Legionary's Checklist:

- ☑ iron or bronze helmet
- ☑ body armour (*cataphracta*), a cuirass tunic of overlapping bronze or iron kilt (*cingulum*), made of hanging, jangling metal and leather straps
- ☑ leather sandals (*caligae*) with hobnailed soles and leather laces
- ☑ shield (*aspis*) made of plywood
- ☑ two javelins (*pilae*) with heavy metal heads
- ☑ dagger (*pugio*)
- ☑ short sword (*gladius*), used for stabbing with its double metal blades
- ☑ leather scabbard to house the *gladius*, which had a wood or bone grip
- ☑ 15-day supply of grain
- ☑ cooking pot
- ☑ two stakes for building up palisade fencing to surround the camp
- ☑ basket
- ☑ pick
- ☑ double-headed axe (*bipennis*)
- ☑ saw

Today's modern soldier – in full kit – carries about half as much in weight as a typical Roman legionary.

Roman legionaries weren't given just military training – they were taught skills like engineering, building and surveying so that they could build their own defences, forts and camps.

Roman soldiers fought hard in battle – but so would you if you knew what the Romans did to troops who failed. Units considered to have been cowardly or who ignored orders were punished. Lots were drawn, and one soldier in ten was clubbed to death by the other nine, not-so-friendly, fellow soldiers.

Centurions in charge of platoons of Roman soldiers used a vine staff both to show their rank and to keep discipline. One officer was known to his troops as 'Fetch me another', because he broke so many vine sticks thrashing them.

Caged Money

Roman soldiers made themselves a special money cage out of bronze wire, which they fitted inside their mouths as they went into battle. Pliny the Elder records several instances of centurions getting so carried away as they stabbed their victims in battle that they yelled out – and as a result swallowed their money cages!

'Oh, dear – that doesn't taste so good.'

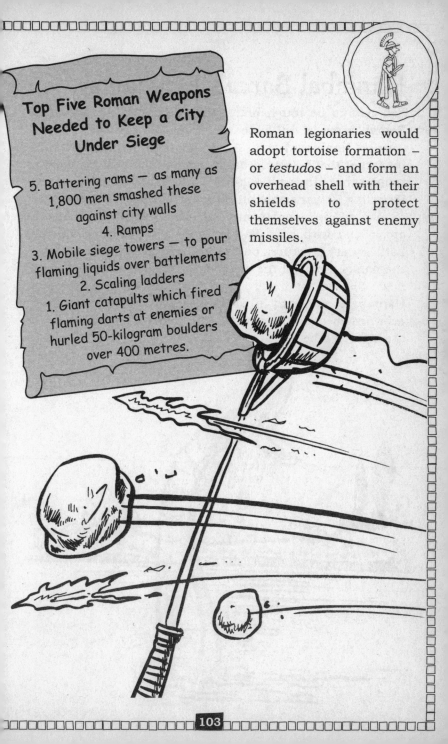

Top Five Roman Weapons Needed to Keep a City Under Siege

5. Battering rams — as many as 1,800 men smashed these against city walls

4. Ramps

3. Mobile siege towers — to pour flaming liquids over battlements

2. Scaling ladders

1. Giant catapults which fired flaming darts at enemies or hurled 50-kilogram boulders over 400 metres.

Roman legionaries would adopt tortoise formation – or *testudos* – and form an overhead shell with their shields to protect themselves against enemy missiles.

Hannibal Barca's Elephants

You had to be tough and totally dedicated to take on a Roman army in full force . . . A bit like Carthage's finest warrior, Hannibal Barca. Aged only nine, he had sworn to his father that he would battle against Rome all his life. No wonder that, during the Punic Wars, Hannibal led an army, including 50 war elephants, over the mountainous Pyrenees to take on his hated enemy. Faced with the River Rhône to cross, and with only 37 elephants left, Hannibal led the battle-weary creatures on to rafts, which he cut loose from the banks. Some of the elephants panicked as they floated down the river and overturned the rafts. Although some of Hannibal's men died in the proceedings, not one elephant drowned, because they used their trunks like snorkels in order to breathe.

Five Problems the Romans Faced When they Attacked the Greeks at Syracuse (213 BC):

1. catapults that threw stones weighing over 370 kilograms, which made splinters out of Roman battering rams
2. wooden beams which extended from the city walls out over boats in the sea, so that the Greeks could drop huge pieces of rock and lead to sink the Roman ships
3. a pulley system of grappling hooks that overturned ships or smashed them against rocks
4. a pulley system of grappling hooks that hoisted Roman soldiers up into the air, before letting them drop to their death
5. small catapults, used by the Greeks to fire lead darts at attacking Romans.

DID YOU FIND THAT FIB?

13.
Roman Leaders

There were some very important people in Ancient Rome. Some of them are remembered to the present day, on account of the things they did – for good or bad! But can you work out which is important and which is the fib?

Julius Caesar (Ruled: 47–44 BC)

Julius Caesar, the original 'Roman Geezer', became so well respected that many of his troops offered to serve in his army without pay. And, when food and supplies were non-existent, they survived by eating grass. The troops had every reason to be tough in battle, however. Clever Julius had given them gold and silver weapons so that they wouldn't give up their precious swords without a fight.

When Julius Caesar chased his Roman enemy, Pompey, into Egypt, Julius was given a gift of a rolled-up carpet. When he unrolled the carpet, he was surprised to find:

(a)
Queen Cleopatra;
or

(b)
12 poisonous asps;
or

(c)
the heads of his slaughtered troops.

BEST SURPRISE

Answer: (a). Not only did Caesar unroll Cleopatra, famous queen of Egypt; he was surprised to find that she was stark naked! And he hated the pattern on the carpet!

Augustus
(Emperor: 27 BC–AD 14)

Julius Caesar's great-nephew, Augustus, was the first and greatest Roman emperor. He succeeded in replacing the Roman republic with a system of monarchy, headed by emperors.

Augustus had such a hatred of beards that he used to order his slaves to shave him at least 12 times a day. They were also ordered to shave every hair off his head. If Augustus spotted anyone in the Senate buildings sporting a beard – whether a goatee or full-grown – they were levied a 'Beard Tax' of 12 *denarii* on the spot. Or, rather, on the beard!

Caligula (Emperor: AD 37–41)

This emperor's name was really Gaius – 'Caligula' was just a nickname, meaning 'Little Boot'. He was known for being . . . well a bit on the bonkers side.

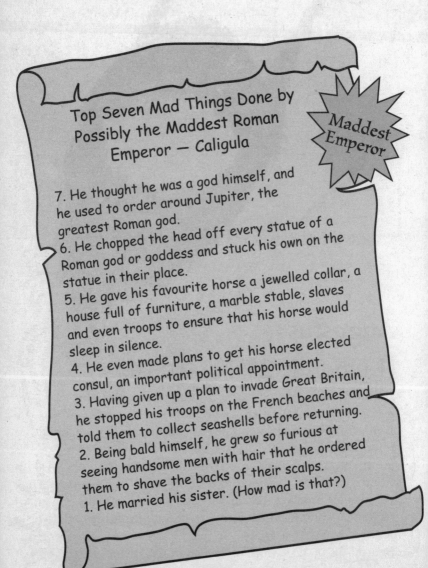

Top Seven Mad Things Done by Possibly the Maddest Roman Emperor — Caligula

Maddest Emperor

7. He thought he was a god himself, and he used to order around Jupiter, the greatest Roman god.

6. He chopped the head off every statue of a Roman god or goddess and stuck his own on the statue in their place.

5. He gave his favourite horse a jewelled collar, a house full of furniture, a marble stable, slaves and even troops to ensure that his horse would sleep in silence.

4. He even made plans to get his horse elected consul, an important political appointment.

3. Having given up a plan to invade Great Britain, he stopped his troops on the French beaches and told them to collect seashells before returning.

2. Being bald himself, he grew so furious at seeing handsome men with hair that he ordered them to shave the backs of their scalps.

1. He married his sister. (How mad is that?)

Nero (Emperor: AD 54–68)

Nero was only 16 when he became Emperor of Rome. His taste for power went to his head and he became a hated ruler, even burning down the city of Rome in AD 64 and then rebuilding much of the city as his own 'Golden House'. When he toured Greece, the Olympics were run just for his benefit and – big surprise – he won every race in which he entered!

Nowadays, we talk of a time-wasting activity as being like 'Nero fiddling while Rome burned'. However, he couldn't have fiddled whilst Rome burned, as the violin wasn't invented until centuries later.

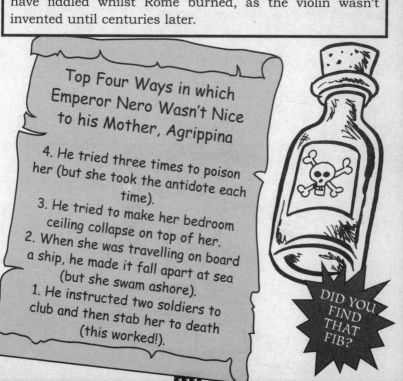

Top Four Ways in which Emperor Nero Wasn't Nice to his Mother, Agrippina

4. He tried three times to poison her (but she took the antidote each time).

3. He tried to make her bedroom ceiling collapse on top of her.

2. When she was travelling on board a ship, he made it fall apart at sea (but she swam ashore).

1. He instructed two soldiers to club and then stab her to death (this worked!).

DID YOU FIND THAT FIB?

14. Find That Fib... Answers

Chapter 1. Life and Death in Ancient Rome

If you believed that trumpet-playing stilt-walkers took part in Roman funerals, then sorry – I'm afraid you've been taken in by a Fantastic Fib.

However, in truth, an important Roman funeral procession wasn't always a sad affair. The mourners often hired clowns to fool around and make jokes about the recently deceased family member. This clowning was meant to remind everyone that even the great were only human.

Chapter 2. Rome wasn't Built in a Day

It's not very fashionable to believe all that nonsense about young girls falling off a narrow walkway during fashion shows in the Forum – that was totally made up.

However, the Forum was undoubtedly an important place, being the economic, cultural and political centre of Ancient Rome. From 54 BC onwards, Julius Caesar demolished the old Forum which was built on a drained marsh, and started constructing some impressive buildings, including the great Basilicas of Aemilia and Sempronia, and the Arch of Titus.

Chapter 3. Times of the Day and Year

If you didn't believe the bit about wearing a fish, lobster or crab on your hat during the annual Festival Of Libertarius Maximus, then good for you – you Found That Fib!

However, the Romans really did celebrate the Festival of Fors Fortuna every year on the 24 June on the far bank of the Tiber. It was a day of picnicking on the riverbank and sailing up and down the river in small boats. A bit like the regatta at Henley-on-Thames – only with sacrifices to the goddess Fortune!

Chapter 4. Growing Up

If you knew we were making up the Favourite Games for Boys and Girls involving sacrificing hamsters and dressing up as goddesses, then congratulations, because you Found That Fib!

However, it has been established that the actual Favourite Game Played By Roman Boys was pretending to be a Chariot Driver in a model chariot attached to a goat. Whereas, Roman girls' favourite game was playing with rag dolls.

Chapter 5. Ye Gods

If you believed that paragraph about a Roman god being called 'Untidius' was rubbish, then well done – you Found That Fib!

However, Romans did undoubtedly have two types of gods – ones who looked after the state, and ones who looked after the family – and they worshipped both with equal vigour.

Chapter 6. Superstitions and Making Decisions

Now, if you chose not to believe that story about Roman soldiers seeking good luck by spearing frogs with one quick spear stroke before sticking them on their belts, then lucky you!

However, care had to be taken during any animal sacrifice in Roman times. If a beast was half killed, or even if it ran away during the sacrificial ritual, this was considered to be an extremely bad omen. When it happened to Vitellius as he was preparing to fight at Mevania in AD 69, he took the hint and scuttled back home to Rome!

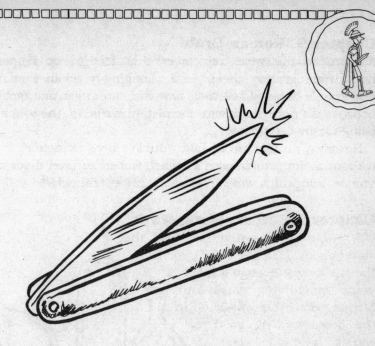

Chapter 7. Amazing Inventions

What's that? You didn't believe the story about inventor Julius Produs Minimus and his combined knife, fork and spoon? Well, you are right!

Mind you, the Romans did invent the world's first steel knives, which they used for shoemaking and other tasks. Then, in AD 1, they cleverly came up with the first folding knives.

Chapter 8. Funky Fashion

If you didn't believe that Roman would-be politicians wore bright, tie-dyed, pink, orange or purple togas, then go to the top of the style stakes! That fact is false.

However, Romans who canvassed for office did actually wear a special *toga candida* – a garment made white by having pipe-clay rubbed all over it. That's why they were called *candidati* or 'whited men'. Oh, and being politicians, they had whiter-than-white reputations anyway . . .

Chapter 9. Roman Grub

A word to the wise: remember that fact about Roman housewives grating cheese and chopping vegetables on a centurion's breastplate? Well, now you can forget that fact – because it's not true. It was completely made up – as well as being totally unhygienic.

However, no Roman kitchen would've been complete without an implement with a raised, ribbed surface, made of bronze, and which was . . . er . . . great at grating!

Chapter 10. Work, Work, Work

OK, admit it. You never believed that story about Manlius Scipio focusing the sun's rays through a home-made magnifying glass and burning down his workshop in the process. Well, good on you as I have to tell you that it was totally made up!

However, in the last century BC, Roman glassworkers discovered that it was possible to blow glass and so make all sorts of vessels. This meant that glass bottles, jars and flasks were mass-produced quickly and cheaply, using special moulds.

Chapter 11. That's Entertainment

If you reckoned that Roman gladiators never wore armour made from the shell of the giant land tortoise – then congratulations! You Found That Fib!

However, some gladiators really did wear gold-coloured armour, studded with precious gems and decorated with ostrich and peacock feathers . . .

Chapter 12. Wars and Battles

If you believed that Roman soldiers made special cages out of bronze wire which fitted inside their mouths and helped to keep their money safe, then I'm afraid you were taken in by the fib.

However, Roman soldiers really did keep their money safe during battles by putting it in bronze purses that looked like bracelets and fitted on their arms.

Chapter 13. Roman Leaders

If you disbelieved that stuff about the Emperor Augustus and his hatred of beards, then well done – you Found That Fib!

However, it is a fact that most Roman men went through life clean-shaven, until the Emperor Hadrian grew a beard to cover up a scar on his cheek, and so his loyal Roman subjects copied him and started growing beards as well. However, the fashion was reversed by Constantine, who made it trendy once more to be clean-shaven. Romans never copied the fashion of their enemies, the Celts, who wore just a moustache.

Puffin by Post

Know-It-All Guides: Conquering Romans – Nigel Crowle

If you have enjoyed this book and want to read more,
then check out these other great Puffin titles.
You can order any of the following books direct with Puffin by Post:

Know-It-All Guides: Incredible Creatures • Nigel Crowle • 0141319775	£3.99
Flabbergasting facts to impress your friends!	

The Time Wreccas • Val Tyler • 0141318570	£5.99
An exciting fantasy adventure that takes place in a world within our world	

Dazzling Discoveries • Mary and John Gribbin • 0141319720	£6.99
Fascinating trivia and far-out facts	

Artemis Fowl: The Opal Deception • Eoin Colfer • 0141381647	£12.99
'Wickedly brilliant' – *Independent*	

How I Live Now • Meg Rosoff • 0141318015	£6.99
'A crunchily perfect knock-out of a debut novel' – *Guardian*	

Just contact:

Puffin Books, C/o Bookpost, PO Box 29,
Douglas, Isle of Man, IM99 1BQ
Credit cards accepted. For further details:
Telephone: 01624 677237
Fax: 01624 670923

You can email your orders to: bookshop@enterprise.net
Or order online at: www.bookpost.co.uk

Free delivery in the UK.
Overseas customers must add £2 per book.

Prices and availability are subject to change.

Visit puffin.co.uk to find out about the latest titles, read extracts and
exclusive author interviews, and enter exciting competitions.
You can also browse thousands of Puffin books online.